Printed in the United States

ISBN: 978-0-692-15912-5

Book cover and logo design by Aqeel El-Amin

Counter Space Gallery www.counterspacegallery.com

Blessed and Thankful
for all of my family and friends
Who have been at my
front, back and sides
During this journey we all call life.

I only pray that I will inspire my
children
To follow their dreams and
Turn them into realities.
Ishmael, Idreis, Inayah,
Ibrahim, Isa and Inara,
I see so much clearer
with you, my six "I"s.
Your possibilities are endless.

Peace and Love are tangible

Artists in order by name:
Jesus Arangure
Myles Cordae
Aisleen Mayfield

Editor:
Flory Sommers

Sections

Contents

This project
Is a
Triangular Renaissance
Where:

Art

Poetry

&

Music

Meet to form
A magical collaboration

The journey is
So much better
With you all at the
Vertex.

Everything
I
Am

•

Jessica Winnie

Discovering

I was afraid to pick up the
pencil
What truths would
Bellow out from the lead
If I began to write?
The word beckons sincerity
To make itself be seen on
paper.
It is there within
The flesh of my script
That I became aware of self.
All that I am not
The soul I strive to be

My Poetry

It's my pretty painted picture

I don't need a pen or pencil to write

just say what's on my mind
            and hope that it rhymes

really don't matter, if it don't tho
            you see, cause it's

My Poetry

my thoughts

my feelings, how I choose

to say it, relay it
            some people even spray it
                    we call that graffiti though

words with meaning on a wall
            an art form
                    just like
                            My Poetry.

So ima pick up my can

Spray my words down on paper

create a Mona Lisa

my own original masterpiece

for all the world to read
            cause it's

My Poetry

Prolonged Penetration

Picked up this pencil,
the Lead spoke,

Said, "Where you been ?

Missing "us",

Let's arouse these words."
So I laid on the mattress, let my expressions flow.
Shared my inner thoughts,

the secret places seen.
Pouring out my soul,

revealed the distant dreams.
Watching the way we grow,

in a rhythm of relief.
Sensual spots touched as I
wrap my fingers around and grip.
In between the lines where I open up,
not afraid to be, the giving all of me
making sure to dot every eye, as you cross the tee.
Keeping the marginal lines intact.
Utterly put it down on you like the truths

that roll off my tongue.
Caressing this paper with a number two
Pen feeling jealous, wanna be the One.
Beside ecstasy a point, which remains sharp
putting pressure on broken down wood

Now slowly... Let it out... Breathe in...
Exhale.
Reunited and it
feels so good.

See I'm Changing

This fall is more than transformation
Truly my season.
Countless reasons of manifestation
Infinitely teeter totter
Themselves through the highs and lows
Oncoming full Libra moon
Water levels that engulf this earthly
Shell I adorn
Replaying the balancing that had occurred
As the skies change
With dusk ying yanged to dawn
Overwhelmed with gratitude
The inner tide heaves and hoes
As harmony sways
retracting and forth going
Cause the valley
Was worth every salt water droplet
To see the stars shine at the peak
Of this mountain of mine
Learned long ago to keep climbing
Rising to The Top
October eighteenth
Nineteen seventy six
This little
Light of mind

Pretty Girls

Pretty girls don't cry
Ain't that a lie
spent the day on my side
and they ran so fast
down my cheeks
I thought for a moment I may have
Slobbered in my sleep

Beaming teeth only display themselves
When unconsciously in REM's state
Recalling when love felt like Fate's first date
happiness in motion
waking up from sleep
with only my dreams
but you gone.

Now Reality,
So...
only see you
when I slumber.

Foundation on momentarily
never could detect the bags
from tears escaped
Covered up so
I can begin the day.
We pretty girls
Cry

All the time

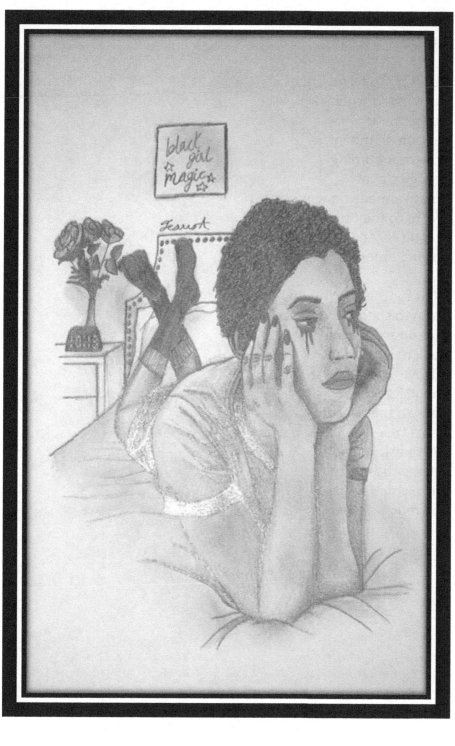

Loose Lips

Don't try to fill my shoes,
get a pair of your own.
Half grown
No time to moan
your feet burning
trying to beat
what I already done won
wrote to the Game
and he called
the next morn

Do it for the charm
learn to spend time alone
pick up the pieces
back to loneliness
Til love
found its way home
back to the heart that
beats to a slow pitter patter
might ask yourself
what's the matter
close your mouth
too much chatter.

No Shame

And then there's the One
I thought I knew...
face grimaces at the sound of your name..
traces of memories lost in pain,
in actuality, let's make it factuality.
dying internally to stay alive, on the outside,

where made up faces

hide the guilt of burdens not barred
allowing lust to sit on doorsteps,
gazing through peep-holes unwilling to open doors.

Swept under mats, not welcome anymore
no longer allow touching of souls,

the way lovers once coiled bodies

like locked puzzle pieces,

the joy that came from giggles at dawn,
now turn that smile one hundred eighty degrees
because although loyalty is a three syllable word,
It is only meant for two,

no longer ashamed of foolish acts
awakened with closed eyes to see

trickery at its best
the way deceit smites away at love
last chapter, book closes, placed onto the shelf.
Left to collect the dust
Of your whispers

Thoughts:

Sufficiency

Whatcha know bout that
Mississippi High Yellah
Sun Kissed
Friar's Point Freckled Face
Delta Blues Red Bone
Firewater Moonshine
Curly Locked
Healthy living
Hooch

Red Bone Relic

she said
he gotta love jones
I laughed
quietly inside
didn't know much
bout them light skinned red bones
down south girls like sweet tea
full of sugar, that'll have you
shoot.. reload.. shoot
never miss. When you

pull that trigger
Wind blows secrets unfold in its whispers
safe with her

little brown eyed girl
catches them and tucks
them away inside
freckled face
half caramel burnt
by the sun
twists and twirls
til your toes curl
in the hypnotic daze of those
high Yellah girls

Red Light District

Had to get that sexy back
When he asked
Me, "If I ever?"
Had I, Would I,
Could I put on those red stilettos
He couldn't recall if I
Ever wore high heels
My mind raced back to that time
Standing in line
Rocking them
Stilettos
Not only did I have
Steel toes
My pedi was a shining
When I yelled out,

"What's my name!?"
he replied, "This better be mine!"
So I answered, with a slow wind
In this club, in this club
I just laughed, out loud,
Have to bring that sexy back
When I heard him ask
Did I, ever wear
high heels.

If You Ask

the Blue Room where ain't no blooz like mine
learned how not to let
them take my shine
So I sparkle like a diamond
Three carats
taking out the setting
much too young for the wedding
Ten years passed
finally let it all set in.
Looked six times and it was too late
funny how things happen
Deprived by destiny
I must be the lesson
No longer fight with fate,
when the actions converse, louder than the words
the bullshit gets old
Silence seems like raging echoes,
Continue walking on fire
until the embers get cold.
A solitude that makes
loneliness seem like it has foes
Had a ninety nine
still searching for dollar hoes with
No place to call home.
Keep rising like the super moon
that pulls the tide in
then comes the question, start with a two step,
Reply with my balance
"Come a little closer,"
I whisper softly to him
If you ask me
to, I will.
Blushes.
It'll just take one session

Honey Girl

At first stroke my vibe,
                puts a crick in your neck
Races down your spine
Ripples all through your back

My inner love births itself
Into your determined, stable,
Beautiful Black mind
As my love soothes and comforts you
Your brain starts to unwind

You won't ask for much but my outer touch
Will teach you more than any scholar could learn
In an entire lifetime
As my being caresses your soul
Like that nipple in your mouth
When you were four months old

First contact leaves you in a state of shock
Puts your thoughts in mind cuffs
Leaves you whipped and your body on lock
An aura that reminds you of how things
Used to be naked in our kingdom
Side by side.. you and me.. pure royalty
Come fill me with your seed

Let's continue the prophecy

I am the mistress of fate, The Queen of destiny
Hurry Up Now… Jump On Board Now..
Don't let it get too late

You know, my love, that love that never goes rotten
Surely never forgotten
So strong.. So strong
I'll smoke you up like chronic, in my favorite bong

I am the game you never win
But insist on playing ova' and ova' again
Like that missing piece
      That maze that keeps you lost
I'm on fire, your desire
      Your soul and spirit I'll defrost

Still that puzzle you won't ever put together
So don't ponder don't even try to wander
It would only be a waste
See my heart, It's on that survival chase
I thought you knew I am the woman
Others can only strive to be
Single and Free

And Oh... Oh so love in with me
You know phenomenal Maya, Winnie,

Oprah, Mary, Lauryn, Sojourner, Coretta Scott King
We come from a place called Africa
The Queens

I got that vibe that loves to foster
I Live On
I Stay Strong
And you know I'll always Prosper

Curly Locks

It's called a Natural
Not a nappy head, fuzzy or bristly bush
Wish I didn't have to wait
So long to love them
Runs from the root up
To the cuticle
I'm being me,
it's Beautiful.

It's called a Natural
Cause it belongs
Didn't have to buy it, sew it,
Press it or comb it.
Runs my fingers through
It's mine and I own it.
Nawh, it's not a care-free curl
Yet my curls are so carefree
Let them blow in the
Wind and Be.

Eden

Ran around searching,
skipped and swayed.
Got lost in the garden,
decided to stay.

Settled down at dusk.

Sang the song
Twirled and twirled
Danced under the stars
basked in the moon
to his forbidden tune.

Awoke at dawn.

Kneeled down to pray
the dew on my forehead
Begging me to stay

My side ached a bit,
Looked all around in dismay
couldn't find the serpent.
instead, a mangled bone
in my path's way

To whom did it belong?
Laying lonely on the ground.
Touched my cage
to find it sore,
a healed scar left to adorn

Looked up in the sky
the light engulfed my soul
a weight lifted,
as if I could finally soar
Found the North Star
freedom in sight
So I began my journey
back home

Left the rib in Eden
Don't need it
No more.

Thoughts:

Consciousness

When love calls
Faces shrug
Went from A to Z
Back to A
Libra scales weighing...
Swaying
Wondering why
Didn't you read the
Memo closer
On how to love

Celebrating My

Integrity

New Beginnings

Determination

Evolution

Perseverance

Excellence

Nobility

Decisions

Education

Navigability

Continuity

Endearment

Scripture

Once hustled the best of them
Smoked up the rest of men
then karma found its way back round
So I had to sit my ass on down
found the Queen I was meant to be
Lord found His home inside of me
now I sit up on my throne,
continue this prophecy

Wouldn't call it fate,
just found my soul mate
and raised him to a man.
So I can look into his eyes now
and destiny don't lie y'all.
cause when I do my lips smile
finally like they s'pose to.

Don't matter the road that got me here
had to chin up and wipe away the tears
Remembered why He put me on
the bigger picture
the long roads, the restless nights
they don't matter no more
So much more than wife
a place where

Love meets

Life.

Little Black Book

Found my little black book
had to laugh, then a smile and a smirk,
a grimace, to a scowl
lips turned upright then upside down again
a tear found its way down my cheek
when the memory of true loves' loss
reawaken the broken heart of a teenage love
scribbled names
fake names next to the alias
even found a name without the number
It's a wonder...
still got his twitter some
twenty years later
flipping through pages
travel down memories' lane
reminisce in love's corner

Bubbles

It's really quite simple
if you can open your mind to see
its bubbles bae bee
Dip it in
stir it around, lift your wand
press your lips and blow
floating off into a lifetime
bursts soon as it comes off the
end of the wand then it floats
float Float on…..floats on… float on
Dip it back in, swish it around,
Lift your wand, press your lips and blow
Double trouble when there's two
chase it til you catch it back
on the palm of your hand
follow it round til it pops
in the corner of your eye
sweet stings
Dip it back in, swish it around
lift your wand
press your lips and blow
See then when you
dip it down low
let that beat drip
then ride the flow

Ballad for You

The shank edges its
way back into the flesh
bones not able to protect
the body that keeps me standing strong
My arms, not long enough to reach around
the pain that agonizes my sleep
now found a way back
into my day.

So what becomes of a broken heart?
Mine seems to want
to pump more blood
Find a way to
erase the wrongs
capillaries blocked due to
all the nights I've spent alone

When my control was not involved
the circumstances seem
to plague me now
only wishing I could just
white them out.
Instead of here
singing my song
which is beginning
to look a lot like
his loss

What Becomes

He said, "Life goes on."
So I started to write my own song
Didn't need Mary to

tell me bout life too
Have my own lyrics boo
If you were my mirror
then I can't see
My own reflection
Empty silhouettes staring back
memories of my Geisha face

Tears roll down
black mascara runs around
The perimeter of my lids

Life is about lessons
So I'll be one.
Didn't pass the test
Back to the
drawing board
To illustrate
What love
really looks like

Small Moments of Truth

Realize me just like she

Gazing in the glass

Can't you see

What you're doing ?

She say,

"He got a family"

For an instant didn't even care,

Feel you now.
Skeletons find their way

misty memories

escape into

gray clouds
disguising themselves

as Truth

She say,
            "It's the phone that rings"

Off the hook
            at one a.m.
                  Confrontations known
                        Oh to well
Karma be untamed like that
            when it's coming
                  back 'round.

Let time tell.

Detached Loyalty

Night marauders came in the dark
      Left a knife lodged in my chest
           For love to drain out gradually
               Spent the day attempting to
                    wrench the handle away.

My soul too aches
Although I've been
moved past heartbreak.

This agony like déjà vu,
      when actions speak louder
           Transform words into truths
               The blade lodged deeply
                    felt attached like this before

So I saved myself.
Reasoned and left love to be alone
If you only want to settle

For something.
      How will you stand?

I went beyond the wall

To give you my hand
Opened up my heart without regret

Heard your prayer through the line
      Lost track of time,
          while I let you
             whirlwind my mind.

Your script so deviously considerable
      must be duplicitous.
This can't be Us,
Holding me down.

25

Jamila- The Beautiful Ones

Powder smeared on the glass
Where you cut yourself out
Memories may fade
They never get erased
As each day passes
I swim a little further
Away from your river of sorrow

To call yourself a man
Surely an understatement
As if you have so many tomorrows
When the promise is only for today

Entrusted my womb to give life
With a seed untainted like
Your addictions that dance with the devil
When safety only occurs
with the absence of you
the wind of the willow tree
type of love that blows

a breeze and
you down south
moments when going home
is the only way
to resurrect home
flying fish
gasping for air

Thoughts:

Intimacy

Shades of Me
The scales of existence
Beyond the darkness
Where light shines
A little brighter
Just where
I want to be
Here with You

Tenderness of Touch

Up close and personal in my aura
within this moment that allows
the presence of souls to connect

when simple pleasures become aware
of the energy in the room

beckoning the touch of innocence
                    unaware of actuality
ignoring the situation
because this condition of selfishness
leaves lips soft and wet
temples caressed

The release.

So don't ask becomes don't tell
the glass globe shaken up
when things settle and it all
all falls down

the stillness of lying there in latitude
In a mirage which evokes desire
That cannot be attained
So the yearning

Burns and smolders without pain
Til the Sandman takes the breath away
Candied dreams, sweet like praline.
Enticing embrace
                    To be set free

Sóla hay una mí

The way you smile
Soothing in a way
like a breeze on a humid Southern day
My beat in your heart
your rhythm in my soul
Casting all expectations aside
See what you find
when happiness crosses back and
forth across the threshold
looking into the mirror
as it all unfolds

Words come out so easily
comfort fills the space
once shared with loneliness
that could only call on despair
now running fingers
through soft silky hair
oils soaking their way through
into the lifeline of your skin

imagine the companion
take a ride on this ship
nothing left but time
no point in holding back
take a chance on the possibility
let this occasion slow grind
into the audacity

Watching you
watching me,
in my dreams
I go there to escape the reality
To be on the simple side
of things, even though
we both can't see
still aware of the scenery

Beyond the place
where crave found covet
remain nameless
endure until Love Is...

not just another word muttered
But a cocoon intertwined
where endearment conceives
and wings open up wide
lips flutter, souls fly away
bewitched in this butter

If all I can do is write,
then I freely commit
to do what comes naturally
Give all of my mind
Let this interlude be my temperance
and let my pen do the time.
There is Only One Me.

Parking Lot Portrayal

Play me a song
Put your fingers on
The black and white keys
Let the notes
Make a sound
Like your voice
In the ride
Til the early morn
Keep me dancing
To the beat
Of your headphones on
Lose track of time
When you realize it's dawn
Conversation rocking
All night long

Nola

Misty evening wind gently sweeps
stare into Sade's eyes
seems like she's watching me
sweet Creole praline
tasty like me
Voodoo brew
drunk too much
like night and day
laying next to you
being juvenile

Lights Out

Tongue twisted
Say my name
Getting Spring sprung
Just in time too,
You always cum
Sing that song
Slow like a lullaby
Rewrite the wrong

Alice's cookies enticing me
Slide into the rabbit hole
Come inside, always warm
You'll see with eyes closed
Wonderland, the place to be.

Never on the side
That's for dem chicks
No compromise, lost on that pole
In your mouth like
A C I S S E J
Turned around, flip upside down
Thigh high, energy so alive

On the rise
The mountain peak of ecstasy
Shhhhh…. Now…..Don't speak.
Catch your breath, baby,
Lay your head
Right here on this
Pillow top and rest.

Moonstruck

Do you think you love me, girl ?
Cause this temperature don't lie
Fall asleep, wake up again,
Fall asleep, wake up again

Wrap strong hands around soft thighs
Arise and let it fly

Never knew that love could be
simple like a Nola breeze
couldn't tell words nothing, just
Lay back watch lips smile
Cause it ain't no surprise
Arise and bring the tide

The way fondling fingers find
Temples; stress released
While rubbing tired feet
Encase itself around the brain

In a dream untapped

Do you think you love me, girl ?
Cause this melody is right
Fall asleep, wake up again,
Fall asleep, wake up again

Bodies locked throughout the night
Arise and let it fly

Never knew that love could be
Sleeping soundly with absent penetration
Woke up amazed, untouched and safe
Fulfilled by energies' embrace
Gazing deep into those pretty brown
Arise and bring the tide

The way fondled fingers find
Spine aches set free
Massaging broken backs
Touch that takes away the shame

In a dream untapped

Mistah d Jay

Pushed replay so many times
The melody not engraved
In my veins like my blood pumping
To the beat in vain.
Patiently waiting on your love
Got me singing, "I don't wanna...
I don't wanna I don't wanna..."
Notes fading in the music
Around me like bubbles in the air
Put my wand in my back pocket since
My ass lies there
Listen to this groove
Sweet sounds of memories
Placed on my soul
Can't hardly move in unison
With thoughts of yesteryear
The timeless ticks spent in bliss
Still ain't washed off my cheek from the first kiss
So far away in distance this capacity half full
If that's the rhythm
Then I gladly be the rhyme
Please play my favorite
Song just
One more
Time

Perla

Softly
Smoke rises
Hands exchange an interlock
Gaze slowly
Bodies in shock
By the power of touch

Slow grind on the floor
In my mind
Dancing just for you
Moving to the beat
Of your eyes watching me
Feeling the bass inside my thighs
No longer holding up the wall
Rhythm of it all

Need a new page?
Wanna be your book
Flip through the chapters
Take a look
Fall asleep reading
Under the moon
Wake up early
Feed you with my spoon
Full of sugar

Got my Libra scales
Coming back into balance
Can't keep you off my mind
In this musical melody
Focused on this trance

See you in my daydreams
Trying to telekinesis
You into this reality
Cause your voice is so magical
Casting spells of Yemaya
All over me

Mercury in my house
Wind blows its love around
Expecting the same in return
Harmony brings
Melody to my charm
Which is so soothing to the soul

Found some admiration,
after much consideration
Need to make a declaration
Won't be
Can't
Nothing be
Quick bout this
Rightchea'

Breakfast in Bed

Secret stares passed my way
A smile returned
As images of last night still wander
The sounds of
Moans and groans
Now silenced by the public eye
The embrace that held me tight
Your head between my legs
hickeys on my inner thigh

Now absent

So I wonder...

"Good Morning" greets me
For a second time
Still a good one
In a room
full of people
Alone with
Me and You

Musical

Filling my airwaves
With a melody
That attempted to explain
This love that yearns
For duration and domain

Roberson in my ears
The bounce in my step
Rockin back and forth
Bumpin to the beat
Of the song
In your head
You left
Just for me

Lyrics tell a story
From beginning
Never say
Good bye
It's just
Til we meet again
Won't ever be an end.

This mix goes on and on
The beat intertwines
Inside of my scales
Balanced briefly
Eyes closed,
Moving my soul

Retracing every stride
Now turned into miles
Where our footprints
Enjoined along the road

Giving the gift
Of musical retreat
Put it in
Press play
Eject
Take it out
Put it back in again
Press play

Wandering

Remembering
When the ocean finds its waves up
Onto the shore
As the tide find its way
Back home
Paused for a moment
Seventh heaven rolled its way on in
Blinked too fast and the dawn
Swept you out again

Thoughts:

Betrayal

Too Many
Can't Get Rights
Wanna Be Wrongs
What is it?
That you Want
From A
Sistah!

Pallet of Proportions

Wonder for a minute
Then I blink me eyelids
For an extended period
While they're closed
I recalled why
I feel that way
That I do
In the first place
Exhale
Picture painted
Paints been dry
So……
Why ask why?
keep it moving

time don't lie.

Popped

My sentiments are not exact
This new day has me feeling
A little bit like
If you not giving what
I need to be intact
When I want..

how I want..

as I want..
Somebody else will.
But then I'm thinking bout you
When I'm with them
They calling and I'm wishing it was you
But I'm on your time, when
I'm supposed to be the dime
I realize that I am very spoiled
I don't like to wait,
Never been one to beg for dates
So if this is a taste of patience
Like a spoonful of sugar
I'll let it go down.
Moments like tonight
When the Bubble got
The game twisted and tricks are for kids
She wants to display what happens
When you blow
I lost my wand in the sauce tho'
So soon as I find this
Mutha fucking rabbit
I'ma get my Bubbles back
Let go of this communal habit.

Yes

I must confess minds telling me yes
Ever since I rested my lips upon your chest
Confusion got me going
On one of those wild rides
Makes me wanna hold on
You know that ride the kind you wanna jump on
Bud up to the front of line on... Ride on
Let it race down your spine and ride on, ride on.

I got this crazed situation
Mad confrontation
Gotta wipe off my forehead
So much perspiration
Just wanna lay down wrap my body surround as
You turn around this frown
Put your head on my breasts
Lay your cheek on my thigh and rest
Soak you up, end this stress
Let me ease into your body hold your soul in
The palm of my hands
Maybe even make you my man
We can always compromise,
But for now, sit back, and let this temperature rise

Can't pinpoint this one
Seemed as natural as the rising sun
At first only an imagination
Never thought it would be done
And now our day has begun
Caught myself daydreaming bout you
The feeling was kinda strong
I guess I never realized it could ever be wrong.
Sitting here restless

Can't get you out my mind
I'll see if you're about
Something real in due time

Don't want to be just a broad that you knocked
Don't want to feel like I'm on your clock
Just don't wanna make it a sex you up thang

It's my heart that needs the orgasm
Make me sing !!
A 60 second, body locking, back breaking fuck fling
A do me baby bump' n grind
Is the last thing I need It's my soul I want you to feed
Not the honey in my panties

Just want you to listen while I'm talking
Run while I'm walking
Be there when I need someone to be jocking
It's you that I want to lock-in
Deep inside the inner depths of me
Can you feel it? Do you see?

Feel like this one is out of my hands
Out on a limb Somewhere…
someone has a master plan
Outta my control….So….
I'ma just lay back and go with this flow
Listen to our rhythm as the bass blows
On and on into the night
We both know this melody is right
And this vibe.. this vibe is Oh so right
Like an angel in flight,

I'm listening, I must confess.

I'm listening to my mind
It's telling me Yes

Karma Cum Back 'Round- Reverse Poem

She's at it again.
Didn't matter if it was
a long time friend
a one night stand
her husband

Bae
or the boyfriend
Coulda' been the boo
the one for you,

doing things
questioning being
feeling unlike the

Who does that ?!

Ohhhhh…

Shhhhh…

Does what !?
I thought you knew
Dip It in put It back in

Only one for me

Shoulda' not been the fool
his wife
had a girlfriend
Side chick too

a little more better, makes it mo' bettah…
a soul mate til the end
Didn't matter if it was
He's at it again
(Re-Read from the bottom to the top)

Cycling

Could answer that
In so many ways
Gonna let it ring
Not off the hook
Cause you ain't
Never being ignored
Always have a place
Warm and cozy
Part-time,
On-Time,
My-Time
Just don't get
How I still find
Myself Alone
Now I know why Stevie
Did so much Wonder
?

Long Pull

If I take it to the head
The explosion
Like a one man sniper
The ridicule surely
Cannot prosper
Take that paper clip
Untwist the pain
Stick it in the pipe
Til it's clean, a gain.
There is a light at the
End of the tunnel
If the flame too bright
Soul don't feel right ?
Then blow that end
Into my mouth,
Lips wrapped around
Shot gun to the head
No rings needed
Til death
We don't part
Meet you in that special place
Only one way to get there
Let that smoke
Keep rising
To the Top.

Boiling

Poured myself in
Simmering
Caught in
A vicious cycle of
Choice
Our indecisive intimate ways
The way we loved
The role I played
In the demise of Love

Turn Around

Flip that W
Back around
Open your eyes
Cause some times
I got to fall in love
First with Me
So even when it's BLIND
You can still see

Silhouette

Love ain't never did me wrong.
realize now that
it was you all along
See, when the words
came outta my mouth
It was true, I love you.
Not the you, the man
in front of me
But you, Love.
Too much to embrace
the disgrace
I sometimes carry
haunted by dust swept under rugs
Love didn't hurt
or lie, or cheat
displace trust, betray or deceit
That was you
Love aches its way through souls
to display
true colors thru the face of another
trying to find itself
It wasn't the Love for
You
that I loved
It was the Love in you,
Loving me back
Because I do love you,
Luv.

Lotto

Siszy...

you gyrate that roulette
And I'll scratch the back
One of us got to hit
that million

Jack!
Kettle calling the tea Black
Worried bout if I'll Fall

losing an hour
Feel like I'm getting one back
Springing forward
Getting these fangs
outta my mutha
fucking
Back

No Change for the Weary

Eye didn't know
Falling felt like this
Until picking my soul
Up as I witnessed her laying
On the ground
Heard a whisper say,
"Let Go"
Love not welcome
Hear no more
Tick Tock
Scales tipped time
Mic drop

Clock stops
Ten dimes
Put them in
My pocket
To keep it one hundred

Tick Tock

Back in the cut
Corner posted up
Watching the room
Til you notice
Finally decide to
Smoothly make your
Way over
After greeting the
Bandwagons
An attempt to say,
"Hello, looking fine in that dress tonight."
Eyes rolled from the simplicity of manners
Mistaken for attention
Breeze blew by then out again
Feeling like you lost that moment?
Sitting in them shadows
of your mind
Trying to get her
Out of your thoughts
Picturing her lips
Glistening in the dim lights
Standing there alone
Cause you
Wasted her
Time

Thoughts:

My branches reach out
The leaves webbed
Like a frog
Ever so green
Bark covered with moss
The shade in my willow
The roots grow deep
My Poet Tree

Baby Kisses

Rocked and Hummed
Her to Sleep
Precious in a way
That Angels understand
Her calm soul
I soaked in
The sweet smell of life
Unconditionally loveable
I have been renewed

Suns

I didn't know my father,

like I know my sons,

so I strive in life

to make sure they learn how to be one.

Raised to be a woman because of my mom

It was auntee who taught me how

to be a black sun, queen amongst some,

So I know not to compromise

Just rise and rise and

Rise

Love and Healing

No disrespect
Cause a life at
Conception is
The miracle
The cleansing of souls
Is occurring
The lost will be found
In the after life
Come willingly or
Unwillingly
Surely you will come
The dead walking amongst us
Being called home
A purging
Beyond the reach
Of humanity's
Perceptions
When prayer is
No Longer
Enough

LIBRAS

Levitate to higher grounds

Where understanding occurs

Invasively intentional in thought and action

Brave enough to endure
the battle scars

Relaxes under the moon
in peace and harmony

Always thinking ahead for our next move

Simple things that make loving easy

Nasir

For a moment in this night hour
I was defeated
Just for an instant
So I cried
Then I looked up
Remembered to strive for perfection
In his eyes
The signs floating above us in the sky
Willingly or unwillingly
Come
So I took another step towards myself
Wiped my cheeks on his shoulder
Recalled why
I named him
My Protector

Twilight

Walked through the thousand grains

Let the Atlantic run in between my toes

Watched the ancestors dance across the waves

Let the rays shine down on my soul

Whispered my secrets to the clouds,

> in hopes that they would

> > blow away in the wind.

Let the West coast breeze hit my face

Wondered if he would ever love my silhouette

Let the seagulls sing my favorite tune

Waited for the sun to set across the horizon

Let the moon push and pull the tide,

> In hopes that it would

> > Balance me under

The stars.

Poppa Hank

See I believe in the numbers
They never tell a lie
seven plus two equals nine,
just like seven take away two makes five
so I guess the stars were aligned when
heaven called him back cause
He would have been ninety-five

The Libra in me had to touch
the other side of life
His body warmer than the
Way the negative temps had
Left my hands.
I tucked them under his shoulder
Put my hands over his

Kissed his forehead and said goodbye

Some say the soul stays within the host
Even after the heart decides to stop
So I breathed in his essence
In hopes I could inhale
Any bit of himself left in that room

It was winter when he left us
Yet the star was shining bright
A blinding type of ray that
Only pearly gates could create

I pulled the shades open slightly so
The light could reach his face
His love for the sun, reminding his earthly body
It was time to go home.

Six days prior Sister Solstice showed her face
So our days not so long
Fajr comes a little earlier in the morn
Memorial still weeks away
Black shawl posted on the door to mourn
Cause he'll be gone for forever,
Gone for forever

Kiss my gramma tell her that we love her

Not supposed to cry cause it makes
the traveling soul sad
So my tears duck behind my lids
conversation confuses the soul
So mental dialogue is a no-no
Just gotta learn to let it all go
When where you are is where we all strive to be

As I search my mind for memories
Of when I was a kid
Lay my head down at night
Waiting for you to come in my dreams
where selfishness meets gratitude
faith finds itself in between

And this life
                    this sweet sweet life

                              Is surely, what is seems.

The General

I found myself standing
Giving an ovation
Accepting that defeat
Was ticking closer
The sound of my hands
Clapping together were
Louder than the two full bands
That surrounded me on both sides
Our eyes met
Chin Up.
Our silent sign language
You confirmed with the usual signal
A nod... Although this one a bit different
Yet still with seconds
Remaining, the personal desire
To compete never
Evaded your body
There I stood, I felt alone.
In a gym full of hundreds
The courts flashed
In unison before
My very own eyes
Clapping to my own beat
For my own son
With admiration and melancholy
Congratulations
To my Royal
My own
Number One

Southside Nights

Love his fingers on them strings
The melody he brings
The sound of chords
As they dance their way
Into my ear drums

Birthday Wishes

The ripples on the water
Like my soul spreading
Into another year
Of life.
Silhouette of self
Not afraid of seeing myself
In the reflection
Cleansed by the
Ocean's sunset

Baby Girl

Laid there and cried
Said, "Momma, look,
I don't have my daddy's eyes."
As she stared back into mine.
Haven't seen him
Since I was three years young
Got a picture... Is it him?

I'm just not so sure. Still searching for a
Father's love in the faces of men

Momma shook her head bout the lies she told
Didn't wanna replay
The night she was a horror.
Seemed simple to say
That he was the father
He came around enough... why bother
With the truth
She might as well been his daughter
One lie leads to another.

Now sixteen, so I guess
I gotta tell her

Come here baby girl
Momma got something to say,
"That man you call daddy
Ain't yours, he went astray."

Eyes glanced down towards the empty floor
Daughter whispered softly,
The words began to flow,
"So the stories are true, the ones in the streets,
                they tell about you,
My momma... was a whore."

Jamil

Wrote your name in the first snow
The birth of winter
Each snowflake fell like the first
Yet each unique
As I stepped outside
I thought of you.
How much your momma
Must miss you
I smiled looking up
Into the sky
Watching pieces
Of heaven
Falling

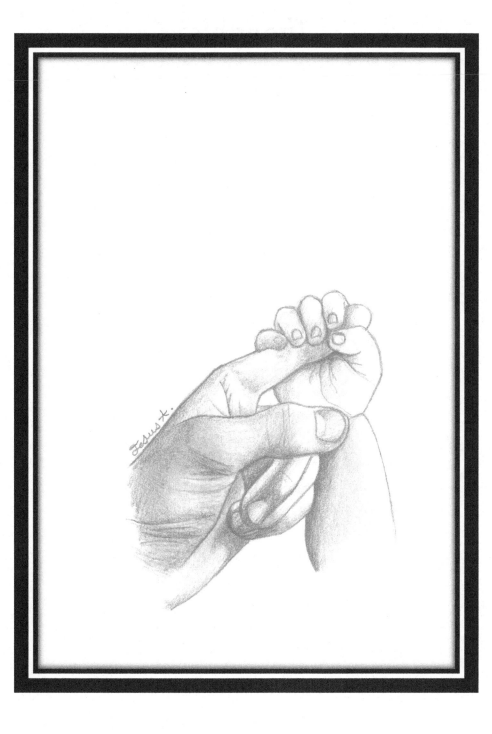

Thoughts:

Race makes
You feel like
Singing
A Sunday church choir
Solo
In front of the
First Family

Grain of Rice

Share the video of a woman being beat
don't matter the shade of skin to me
See we been brutalized since
master woke us out our sleep
the exclamation at the end of the sentence
that is what we're lacking
Amerikkka sensation has rallied once again
flash screen shots of sisters' screams
so somehow the momentum fades
In attempt to disgrace our Kings
unarmed left in the street
code switch maybe then see
we want a little more than change
Now Rice becomes the criminalized
while mothers still weep and our children still die
the click contributes to the dehumanization
Now how we supposed to build this nation?
Actions justified cause Wilson wears the badge
hundreds of our men being murdered
Shot...beaten...choked...lynched
Left for dead..
He left the house for school in a black tee
white words that say "Don't Shoot" me.
I am one who defends the Dream
more than just marching and chanting in D.C.
Before you judge and spread his shame
make sure the kitchen is clean
then don't forget to speak their names
Martin... Brown... Garner... Boyd... Carter...
Sterling, Clark, Bland, Castille,
Reynolds, Brown, Blevins and McDonald
Our millennium martyrs

Happy Holidays

Will you put up a tree?
Hang the names of
The Millennium Martyrs
On the ornaments for me

While Middle Eastern refugees
Turn the other cheek
Going from Inn to Inn
Being shunned and turned away
While little baby Jesus
With his hair like wool
Skin like copper
Lay away in the streets
Like the victims shot

Still watching the North Star
Following it to freedom
Waiting on the Glory to come
Just a tune hummed
Talking bout one day
So we will
Take it as such
Now Let's Begin
This Boycott

Prayer is Not Enough

The numbness has overtaken
        our mental dialect in a
              fashion that
conditions us to
passively persevere
So we would ask the Lord
For a little bit more

        than Grace.

Humbly I
Stand on my feet and pray
'Fore the skin on my knees
Has rubbed off to the point
That they bleed
Begging and pleading for sanity

As the rockets red glare
Don't give me another song
That cries out for freedom
Only meant for my despair
When the sweet Clementa
Surely was not a wretch

If we must wait for love
Let it not be in vain
Clearly the fight against
Terrorism
Begins right here
In our very own
Sweet potato American
Apple pie
Kitchen

Voided Check

How Long...? You said,
"Not Long..."
I can hear Trayvon's scream
Not long?... We waiting
on this spoon fed Dream
Not to sit and eat and shop alongside
For our children
to have some peace
And not be terrorized
on the land our ancestors built
How Long...? Not long!?
Carter.. Not Hova
The one they left hanging in the tree
Not long... We're waiting
Not Martin nor Rodney
Yet another King
Murdered in this
Land of the free
Our Reality

Liberation's Drive By

I close my eyes
Visions
All of us
Boarding on buses
Riding down
On them
Not looking for Freedom
Demanding some
Motherfucking
Justice
Blood curled inside my veins
From the pain
So many signs
So many angels
Showing Us
Time to pick up the baton
That was never handed off properly
Dropped it when we settled
The comfortable rights with
Jim Crow skeletons still
Hung up in the closets
More than just Civil Rights

Black Friday

How about
Be Black on Friday
Boycott.
Not Black the race
Black the Power
In the depths of all of our souls

Be the Blackness when

you close your eyes
and pray for the mothers and fathers
of the slain and murdered men,
women, daughters and sons.

Be the Blackness at nightfall
When cold powerful water was blasted on
Peaceful protests in motion

Be the Blackness of your ballot as
It slid in the electronic machine
and was miscounted

How about Be Black on Friday?

Boycott !

Boycott !!

Boycott !!!

Act like you remember
The Blackness

Sing Sing Celebrate

If segregation was a white wash
Integration was a double cross
Went from sitting in the back of the class
To no child left behind
Yet the achievement gap widens
Where's the growth with time?
More like a debt, owed to generations
Classrooms looking like plantations
Still waiting on reparations

The dream deferred
Never picked up the baton
Just reaped the fruit from the Civil Rights tree
Of sitting in any seat
Now at the lunch counter, still not served
Singing like Starship
We built this country, on sweat and soul.

Never planted our own seeds
After the sixties, now dehydrated
Here in twenty nineteen
No longer strange fruits hanging from trees
Now shot dead in the street, the suffering.

The Dream still alive just like Hope
Getting rammed down my throat so
Much that I just might choke
Wish they would have given us the Mountain Top
A plan to reach its peak
I still salute the King and his legacy
One Man… One Day
Just not enough for me

For Cap

You got that DNA
Same one that ran and told
That Nat Turner was coming.
Stayed and watched Master
Sell away your brothers
Rape your sisters
Until their sons were born
From his bitches' britches.

Bloodline that stretches the soul
Of the Atlantic...
Each angle of the triangle watches
As you trade your entertainment
For your brother's knee
It was a bloody Sunday...
Were you not there when they killed...
Clark, Castile, Blevins
Hand across your heart

Chin up... eyes on the flag...
All together now...
"Lift every voice and sing
Til earth and heaven ring
Ring with the harmonies
Of Liberty."

Alton Serling
Thurman Blevins
Amandou Diallo
Walter scott
Rekia Boyd
Tanisha Anderson
Stephon clark
Tony Robinson
Terence Crutcher
Sandra Blevins
Mark Cla
Philando Castile
Eric Harris
Trayvon martin
Botham Jean
Korry Gaines
Mya Hall
Rodney King
Laquan Mcdonald
Miriam Carey
Nyana Stanley-Jones
7
NEGROES FOR LEASE
Jamar clark
Emmet Till
Yvette smith
Fred hampton
Deborah Danner
Tamir Rice
Charleena Lyles
Mike Brown Jr
40
Jesus b.

Queen Korryn

Our seeds
        Watered with
                the Blood from our tears
Sprouting in this
Amerikkkan nightmare

Activist
        gunned down
                In her home, her son
With his gaze watching God
We keep our

Eyes on the prize

        The promise land

Passing of Batons

It is the new generation
That will give their lives
For the generations to come
While we have enjoyed the fruits
Of the '60s labor
Because numb to the 13th Amendment
Sighed and shook our heads
As the list continues

Now shot dead in the streets
Mommas' souls weep
Wage slaving in the house
Need to be in the field planning
When it burns like Rosewood,
Black Wall Street
must be Reconstructed
The blood flows

onto the pavements
Leaving stains of

insanity and pain

Sterling

When will we say
Enough is enough
Speak it with our pocket books
Credit cards, checks
Most importantly our cash

The patriarchal Masters
Entertained through the
Strongest... Biggest... Tallest
Third and fourth generation
Mandingo warriors

Recollection of the Negro Leagues
Dissolved because the Great Depression
Thought back then
We were in a recession

Black Men still not respected
Takes a ball to be your icon
Put a gun in our hands
Dress us in Black
Shot down... flooded streets with crack

Field hands turned into wage slaves
House hands still waiting at the door to be paid
Running high knees sprinting down the court

While privileged private interest groups
Turn Gangsta Southern East Coast rap
Into the new Triangle Trade
Lumber, Iron, MS25 highways paved
With slavery by another name
Still no shame
1.9 billion in his pocket
Trade the trade.

God forgive me
If my pen is misled
These words spoon fed
From the fruit of my faith

Pondering acts of terror
When the guided are gunned
Down in the building of the Lawrd

We turn and look way
Only blue-eyed
Badge-wearing Anglo-Saxon
Christians can terrorize
In Amerrikkka today

Ferguson Flaws

The martyr lays marred
the outrage swept under Mastahs' rugs
the tanks fill the streets
in Amerikkka where we free.

The mother mourns.   '

Social media posts become a thread of hate
The martyr lays marred
Hands raised in peaceful retreat
invisible chains on his feet
since when can we not walk
in the middle of the street?
Were you there when they killed...
endless names added to the scroll
another story untold.

The father mourns.

The videos shared breeding pedigrees of hate
Hands raised
The revolution *is* being televised, webbicized,
corporatized, demonized, idolized
the chickens come home to roost
the noose transformed to the trigger
cause he just another...
King from the motherland
stolen, cast away, bamboozled
now the chariot bringing him home.

The country mourns

The blogs become a venue of hate
The Revolution

Original Photo by: Carolyn Yang

The Movement

Requires
You to be
Uncomfortable

The Movement requires you

To spend within your community
To transform your patterns
To live without

The Movement requires you

To recycle your dead presidents
Into hands the shades of yours
To allow difference into your journey
To take up space on the sidewalk

The Movement requires you

To adapt to situations
To amend your life for the revolution
To support Black business

The Movement requires you

To raise your fist for injustice
To exercise your fifteenth Amendment
To be noticed and take notice

The Movement
Requires
You

Thoughts:

Adoration

Left a flower
On my doorstep
Delicately plucked
Its petals
Loves me... Loves me.. Loves
me

Broken Walls

360 degree turns
Til I was dizzy
                As the room
Finally stopped
Spinning and my
View became clear
                        I could see

Again.
So,
I

picked up a pen to write
                It bled out red
Problem was
                        The ink is blue

And so I scratched my head
Love had somehow
Found its way
On through

T.K.O.

Breath birthed life
So why not breathe again
The challenge is not to read the mind
Rather relax and let the brain unwind
Cause with time pain don't just go away
So the things that once hurt, no longer remain
Then care finds its way into

the subtle parts of the day
Tenderness speaks its' name,
The lessons you taught become
The plans that you learned
So admiration becomes less of a confrontation
guard goes down, while the gloves stay on
yet still a smile reminds.
Regrets have no place in the ring
A soft hum that captures eyes
Twinkle back
Written like stars in the sky
To a melody, lyrics that know a

verse written for two
So we sing, one line
in unison
knocked out
by Love

Distant Reminisce

The bliss of our first kiss

Replays in my subconscious

The way your lips cascaded onto mine

An overtaking, reoccurring vision.

Retrospect finds its way into our phantasies

Separates our time

Keep my eyes open, so I can see the reflection

Of yours in mine

That night on the patio

Where simple hand shakes

Turned to late night phone dates

Like we was back in high school

Neither the fool.

For when love knocks

Peeking through the keyhole

With my foot in the door

I gladly, yet cautiously

Very slowly open

As long as it's *you*

        standing there

                in the foyer

On the 14th Day

Don't need no Valentine.
I know he mine
Not just my Boo nor Bae
Treats me three hundred sixty five
Get it always... in all ways.
Not bamboozled for a day
He settle on my spine.. the melody we make
give me that slow wind with Marley in our backdrop
Throw it upside down like that pineapple cake
Let it pop,

      make sure I stay on top,

              like a Queen Bee Boss.
Later for the lobster date
I'll take that yummy yummy sauce.
Like that lemon sting
in my sweet tea, cause it do make me swing
let that thang... Do its thing!
When it ring... let it rang!
Til the soul learns to sing...
Do whop do whop do whop do-aaahhhh
Then I call out his name
My Everything.

Love Lines

My warmth when I'm cold

My smile when I am glad
Like a forehead kiss when I need compassion

My umbrella in the rain
Like a roof when I need shelter

My Exchange
My hand in his
        palm.

If my love line
Was damaged
Along the way
on this journey
Surely his healing,
            embrace
                    extended it for
                            A lifetime

My palm in his
        hand.

Bathtub Of Roses

When every petal
Transforms itself
Into a memory
Shared by two
Weary joints rejuvenate
Tender muscles rejoice
Mesmerized in lavender's magic
Laying in all the memories
That make us who we are
Dizziness from the heat
Withstanding all distractions
In this here and now
Peace flickering in cinnamon lights
Luther in the background
No longer alone
Now this bond of H_2O
Our every existence
Floating calmly around my essence
Laughter finds its way into
The echoes of the water's ripple
Til the last bubble pops
Recline into motionless bliss

Thoughts:

Forgiveness

Mountain Top
Been down in the valleys
Crawled, limped, skipped
Walked, ran...
To my Peak
See the sky
So much clearer from
Here

Declawed

Shaking off them crabs
In my barrel
Pushing them knives from
Out of my back
Declawing them monkey hands
From my shoulders
Sweeping all the dust from
Under the rug
Into a pan
Gently placing it into the trash
Because we know
That misery loves company
We let the devil lie
Lay where you may
Stepping over
Being brave
Can't have me no more
Words transformed
Into declarations as
Their eyes were
Watching God, reveal while
Receiving the blessings
Grace and mercy
No longer disguised

Angel Kisses

At times
I sit in the dark
So I can see
The shadows bounce
As the blackness whispers secrets
I listen to the stories
Connecting myself to
The other side
Fearless of
The movements
That beckon me to exhale
Realizing you are always
With me
And so I am

No longer afraid.

Open Doors

The faithful
Take chances
Are optimistic
Believe in the unseen
Trust in their life lessons
Give of themselves to others
Know that through patience
And perseverance
Results will follow
Thankful for my
Opportunities

Storm Lifted

Moon beams
Still shine
Through the clouds' blankets
Covering yet the stillness
That yearns for balance
Pulling the tides
Back yonder so
Peace can find its
Way back
Giving the mind a piece
Of understanding

Zero Degrees of Association

Karma got me in this ring
Good thing
I learned the
Rope-a dope
Some thirty years ago
Know how to flow
With the river that winds
Itself in a 180 degree serpentine
Cause everything you do
Comes back in folds
Learn to let go
So you can grow
Not get lost in these
Twenty four hour
Episodes

Sequential Small Steps

Let me tell the story, sharing my narrative

Telling it often, not just the last chapter
I sit back rocking
back and forth in Grandmother's chair
I watch the darkness
The vices come in multi-delusional
shadows of my doubts
Skeletons get in my way
climbing out of the closet
Attempting to block my progression
I push them
With all my force I repel my magnetism
Step over them
Strength in numbers, consciously counting my steps
Looking past then,
Trying to totally forget the pain
That don't work.
Still searching for the goals
Moving bey...ond
Just what this life's reality shows
Transforming the chances
Speaking my mind in
A way that is out of my
Character
Yet still ready to deal
With any consequences
That come from my choices
Whether they be
Right
Or
Wrong.

94

Thoughts:

Deliverance

Just when the rope
Was shortened
And I'd thought I'd
hung Myself
A voice whispered
You are not alone
It's time to come back home

Miscreants

Look into my grace
While counting the freckles
Hidden within my face
The angel kisses
Covering my skin
For the countless
times I've sinned
Marked with the omen
Disguised by the smile
That welcomes morality
Deep inside the pupils
Where my heart aches

Harvesting the Full Moon

Wish you was here
So we could go
Down by the river
To dance
So we could love in the light
That shines even through darkness
So we could lay down the stones of compassion
Circle it around three hundred and sixty
End up right here together,
Where we started
Forgive those who
Trespassed against love
Pray for those we want to love
And the wisdom to know
What love is and what love is not
Wish you was here
So we could go
Down to the river
And dance

Salt Water Sajdah

At times they fill themselves
Only to fall
To refill
Dripping icicles from the
Roof of my temple
Reminding me the
Road just winds around
Around and over
And under
Beyond my reach
So kneeling seems
The only thing
That comforts me
For it is there
That I know
I will find
Grace

Dottie

Angels speak through strangers
Every day finds a little more courage
Daydream now to find you
No longer here in this space
We are all passing through
To know agony
Yet find peace in thoughts of heaven
The balance
When love hurts so bad
Missing you more
As the days pass on without you
Strength in Scripture
And the Word.

Valentine Shears

Took this day of love
To remind my soul
That beauty is only skin deep
The waterworks that had been held in for weeks,
Would not be released, I chose to remain fierce.

Remembering that my faith gives me strength.

The Lord's love guarantees birth and decease
An everlasting love that forgave me for my past
Never thought twice bout the locks
Once I sat down in her salon chair

Continuously tumbled from my grace,
Running fingers through my hair
letting vanity overcome, blinded like mace
She said a young school teacher now fit my frame
I listen close when the elders speak,
          the journey to free   Finally I
could let go of the shame,
release the times I pretended to believe the lies
the night I laid clench-fisted in the bushes waiting to attack,
The choke that releases, hands that slapped, fists that bruised

the ankle that bleeds
          with each snip of the scissors
                    the pain ceased.

Bellowed out, "This is for you, Love!"
As the inches of hair hit the floor
Run my hands quick now
Don't have to relive the long
Wrap that kept me going in circles
Love for self,
I welcome you back
Gladly open the door.

La Luna 101

Be gracious and humble
Two things I learned to be and do
A little bit more of;
Smile when sadness overcomes
Put memories in place of pain
Give enough back to self in order
To replenish what others took
Smile when happiness overcomes
Put presence in the moment
Live for this day
Never forget to dream
Dance under the moonlight

Uncovering Me

The journey back

to where it all started

when I was stronger than I am now

precious lawrd take both my hands

      more than just a verse in a song
            now a mantra that I hum

in my Delta blues accent
shaking profoundly

as the demon releases my soul

I knew then what I know now
        excuses and justifications

Always

If you know better, then you do better
       this road not less travelled
           now my jihad
             confessions of ignorance for
                 the young lady whose
vices
led to the demise of self
      shook my finger, back and forth
           on this path alone moving
forward
      back to me

Baby Girl's Last Cry

Your blues ain't like mine,
Waiting for the sun to shine
Inside the skies turn gray
Patiently persevering,
Waiting for the things
I'm deserving
Longing for the day
All my worries go away

Don't need to touch you
Or see you with my eyes
Your divinity is
Why my tears cry, then smile,
Frowning back at me

Feel like singing
"Shoo fly don't bother me"
Get that buzzing out my ear
Stop whispering all those lies
I don't want to hear

I need to put on a Mary song
And get to stomping my feet
Testifying up in here
Bout the shit you done to me
Shoo fly don't bother me.

Following me, not allowing me
Rather be striving than denying me
All that buzzing in my ear
Back stabbing, back biting me
Telling me things I don't want to hear

Like I should be on Brewster's Place
Naked in the tub,
Having my hair washed and
My soul scrubbed

Shoo fly don't bother me
Making my skin itch, my nose twitch
Don't you see you're in my space
Touching my face, you wanna feel my grace?
Get yo' ass outta here!!

It takes pain to make things go away
You have to lose your sight to see,
And change ain't always good
But it's sho's what I need

Your blues ain't like mine.

Bathing in my Soul

Went down to the water
Said I'd
              find my soul
Knelt over and

Let it wash me
All my stories there were told
He listened to
              the laughter
Hugged me close through

              the tears
The journey had become so long
Over several years

It seems I forgot where
          I'd been
So I found a place along
The banks
             to whisper
Things I wanted to forget
He spoke softly
When he said,

"Life goes on, my dear."
And so I don't regret
              Wading there.

Cabin Mitigation

Tucked deep inside
The Cairns hold
Memories of the past
When hypnotism was not an option
As the mind plagued tricks
I would take a pen,
Write it down
Nestle the note
Into the hardened sediment
The stones would move as
They ingested the years
The torment of my pain
Not theirs
The wailing rocks, heavy with grief
Erasing the times that
Would hold me back from destiny
As wind blows and the breeze
Carries off the secrets
Into the deep woods of our land
Safe now...
free from those demons
Of my mental psyche

Under the Moonlight

She gracefully walked down
To the river's bend
Three hundred sixty five steps
Counted thoughtfully in her head
Top toed quietly as
Not to awaken the souls
Took out the satin pouch
That grandmother had
Carefully sewn from fawn hide
Placing the smooth
Stones she gathered from
Under the waterfalls
The circle of stones surrounded
A braided strand of
Sweet grass
A curly lock of hair
Two small diamonds
A baby tooth
A hummingbird feather
An Indian head penny
One match remained
In the box
And so she
Struck It.

Thoughts:

Transforming

I was raised by
the best of 'em
Tears left went West again
Saw life, past the strife
No time to lie
With the rest of them
Manifest
Be Destined
Then

Mirror Mirror

I looked in the mirror
Thought I knew the person
Staring back at me
Turned and saw you glaring
Through the other side
Of the glass
Seeing me for
Who I Am

Graduation Day

Miles into a 15k
I finished strong
Came in first then
last because the battle
Was against myself
Crossed the line
Just in time to put on
My cap and gown

Delusional Insanity

Comforted by loneliness
Reminded of silence's sweet sounds
Spun around until dizziness was just an illusion
Realized that it was only a state of mind
Reluctant to find true meaning;
settling for the cycle
That circles in time
until things seem of validity
When scripture meets solace
So souls can save themselves
Serenity wraps around
solitude and
Whispers softly,
"It's only a dream."
Time to set yourself free

Salvation Street

If I had let the trail
Terrify me
Hold me hostage
Hearken to
The skeletons
I would never have
Been able to
Complete this journey
The tribulations that
Attempt to torment
And so as I
Dust the dirt off
From the longevity
Of the road
My smiles
Widen
A little
More

Letting It All Go

When the heaves got dry
she wiped the tears
from my eyes.
Cool towel on my neck,
to help me forget
cause even the devil has regrets.
Carrying me when unbalanced legs
fell from underneath me
Exhaustingly letting the pain exit my body.
With every conscious memory
came a contraction
the jolt from the core of my very existence.
The agony laying below my knees
staring up at me from below on the ground
In a puddle of vomit
the shadows of my past lie there, glaring back,
lurking in the stench.
Hands covered in memories unspoken
circumstances swept under rugs, until now
spewing Lucifer up outta me
Cold sweats surfaced, and she patted
my face with peace
Til I faded off to sleep
Releasing the torment,
Letting Go.

Healing Metamorphosis

Inhaled the fumes
For what seemed my lifetime
The pollution
Eluded its way out of
My pores not before
love became a cancer
Although always taught that
it cures all things
this disease of the heart
I ingested for decades
An inverted benign tumor
Chemo no longer an option
A transformation in living
Would be radiation
New cells would replace
The damaged
I would choose to live
As toxicity slowly
Escaped the scabbed wounds
The healing occurred
In dimensions
Larger than the cave
Forty days forty nights
The valleys seemed everlasting
The peaks only allowed for moments
To breathe in fresh air
Once dawn greeted me
The journey had succumbed
Delivered and restored

Dancing With Destiny

I'm no more
Deserving
Same as the next
Queen
I'm yearning,
The crabs in the barrels, the snakes in the grass
The monkeys on my back
One day I just couldn't
Take it no more.
Prayer became manifesto
Every breath
I took though...
Brought me a heartbeat
Closer and Stronger
To faith full
Then I could finally release
Let it all go.
Inhaled his breath
Let my lungs fill
With his love
Until it flowed through my veins and became
my Essence.
Recalled the lessons
Let the pain lessen
I promised myself
On my knees
Happiness,
Less perfection
Exhaled
All my confessions
Counted

My Blessings

Healing

Beginning yet another journey
Reminded often
Not to stay in the valley too long
For the travel up to the
Top of the mountain
Can sometimes be a triumph
When I end up at this destination
And reach its peak
The jihad of self will be seen
The striving
Will be worth all of the struggle
Because I would have
Found my Soul
There

Thoughts:

Jessica Winnie, born in Minneapolis, MN, raised in Oakland, CA. Returning to the Northside at the age of 5. Attended De La Salle High School where she was expelled three months prior to graduation in 1994. This experience fueled her fire to be a teacher. Pursuing her education, she attended her freshman year at Hampton University in VA, fifteen years later finishing in 2012, with a BA in Education from Augsburg College.

Raising her six children: Ishmael, Idreis, Inayah, Ibrahim, Isa and Inara. In her seventh year of teaching sixth grade in Hopkins, Mn. An entrepreneur, activist and writer. When she has moments to herself you can find her baking, walking one of the ten thousand lakes or spending time travelling. Blessed to see the world, having lived in India, France, Turkey and the Ukraine.

A love for poetry has delivered her here, to this place where she is blessed to be publishing her second book. *Everything I Am* represents a decade of finding her truths. It truly encompasses emotions of devotion, betrayal, love, forgiveness, loss, courage and desire. In its entirety of realness, rawness and redemption, *Everything I Am* takes her experiences, others' stories and our society which in turn delivers a reading experience to which all of humanity can relate.

A place has been left after each section for you to reflect and write as this is a collaboration of inspiration.

Artists' Bios:

Jesus Arangure
Sixteen year old from Hopkins, Mn. Currently in his junior year, attending Anoka High School. A Lover of Art ranging from music to painting. A goal he has is to continue developing as an artist and have his art reflect that growth.

Myles Cordae
A full time Texas based artist with a studio gallery located in Arlington, Texas. Born and raised in the small town of Racine, Wisconsin. His artistic process began in 2011 as a way of dealing with depression. Being an introvert by nature, creating art became his voice.
The majority of his art is characterized by vibrant colors, bold compositions and subject matter. Inspiration comes from love, life, pain and the Black experience.

Aislinn Mayfield
A senior biology major at Carleton College in Northfield, MN, where she also continues to explore herself as an artist. Developing a passion for visual arts, enjoy drawing, painting and dancing!
Her artwork also reflects a reverent attitude toward black bodies and a self-determination. In addition to her love of art, scientific interests include cancer cell growth and cell signaling in the central nervous system.
Thus far, her art apprenticeship at Juxtaposition Arts and health-related internships and cell biology research experiences as a TRIO McNair Scholar have sparked a desire to combine all the aspects that she loves.

A
Special Thanks
To You.

•

For supporting
this project.

Made in the USA
Monee, IL
01 September 2019